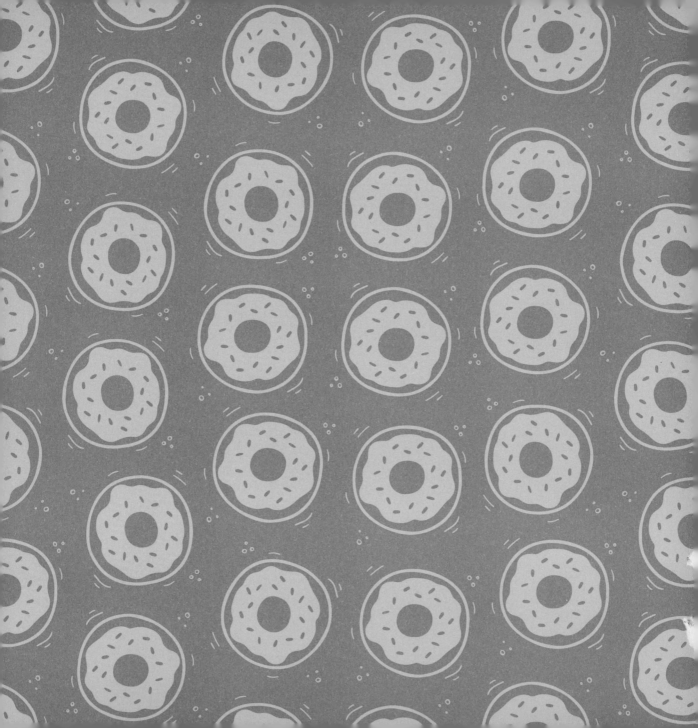

D is for
DONUT

For Hailey and Oliver

Library of Congress Cataloging-in-Publication Data available.
ISBN: 978-1-68555-186-5
eBook ISBN: 978-1-68555-752-2
LCCN: 2022915999

FSC
www.fsc.org

MIX
Paper from
responsible sources
FSC® C102842

Printed using Forest Stewardship Council certified stock
from sustainably managed forests.

Manufactured in China.

Photographs and food styling by Rebecca Wright.
Design by Andrea Kelly.
Some elements licensed from Shutterstock.com.

1 3 5 7 9 10 8 6 4 2

www.craftsncrumbs.com
Instagram: @craftsandcrumbs

The Collective Book Studio®
Oakland, California
www.thecollectivebook.studio

D is for DONUT

RACHEL TEICHMAN

THE
collective
BOOK STUDIO

Of all
the treats
that you have tried,
the best are those
that have been
fried!

First, flour, yeast, and milk
are mixed together and left to rise.
The dough is rolled out and cut,
dropped in oil, and then it fries.

The dough rings are flipped,
and they all cook on top.
When they're done,
it's time to stop.

Take them out of the oil
and give them a little blot.
Now spread on the frosting—
hopefully you add quite a lot!

Then top with sprinkles,
sugar, or coconut.
Did you know donut holes come from
where the donut's shape is cut?

Grab a cup of milk
to dip it in.
A donut for breakfast, or any time . . .

It's always a win!

A is for **APPLE FRITTER**

with fruit and cinnamon inside.

B *is for* **BEIGNET**

it's cut in squares, and then it's fried.

C is for **CEREAL**

crunchy and colorful all around.

D is for **DEVIL'S FOOD**

with dark cocoa that is ground.

E is for ÉCLAIR

topped with chocolate and filled with cream.

F is for FRENCH CRULLER

a special tool shapes it into a swirly dream.

G is for **GLAZED**

covering the bottom and the top.

H is for **HAZELNUT CHOCOLATE**

nutty and creamy, these really pop!

J is for JELLY

which fills this tasty treat!

K is for KEY LIME

citrusy with crumbs, like the pie.

L is for LOUKOUMADES

dipped in honey and piled high.

M is for MAPLE

flavored with fresh syrup from a tree.

N *is for* **NUT**

walnuts, peanuts, almonds—or why not all three?

O is for OLD-FASHIONED

the edges are the best.

P is for POWDERED SUGAR

gets your shirt all messed.

Q *is for* QUICK RISE

for when we cannot wait.

R is for **RAINBOW SPRINKLES**

lots of colors fall on our plate.

S is for **SUFGANIYAH**

filled with jam when they're made.

T is for **TWIST**

it almost looks like a braid.

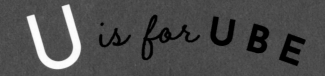

U is for **UBE**

purple yam mash in a dark lavender hue.

V is for VANILLA CUSTARD

piped all the way through.

W is for WHITE CHOCOLATE

covering the fried ring.

X is for X-TRA DONUT HOLES

the thing to always bring.

Y is for YOYO

orange juice goes in the dough at the start.

Z is for **ZEPPOLE**

they're a real work of art!

Donuts are *delish*,
frosted and fried!

So tell me...which ones have *you* tried?

Raised Donuts

Makes about 6 donuts and 6 donut holes

These donuts take a little time to knead, rise, and roll out before they are fried, but it's well worth it for their light and airy texture. You will need a two-quart pot, a cooking thermometer, and a heat-resistant slotted spoon.

For the donuts

½ cup warm whole milk

2 teaspoons active dry yeast

3 tablespoons granulated sugar

1 egg

3 tablespoons unsalted butter, melted

¾ teaspoon pure vanilla extract

¼ teaspoon ground nutmeg

½ teaspoon salt

2¼ cups all-purpose flour

4 to 5 cups canola or vegetable oil

For the glaze

¾ cup confectioners' sugar

2 tablespoons whole milk

¼ teaspoon vanilla extract

Both the Raised Donuts and Quick Baked Donuts can be stored in an airtight container for up to 2 days.

TO MAKE THE DONUTS

1. Lightly grease a medium bowl and set it aside. Line a baking sheet with paper towels and set aside. Line another baking sheet with parchment paper.

2. In a small bowl, whisk together the milk, yeast, and sugar and let sit until the mixture puffs up, about 10 minutes. In a large bowl, mix together the egg, butter, vanilla, nutmeg, and salt. Add the yeast mixture, and whisk until blended. Add the flour and mix until it comes together into a ball.

3. On a lightly floured work surface, knead the dough until smooth, about 3 minutes. Form the dough into a ball and place it into the greased bowl. Cover with a clean, damp kitchen towel and let rise until it doubles in size, about 30 minutes.

4. Turn the dough out onto a lightly floured work surface and flatten it lightly. Roll out the dough until it is about ¼-inch thick. Using a donut cutter or two round cookie cutters, about 3 inches and 1 inch in diameter, cut out the donuts and donut holes.

5. Pour about 2 cups of oil in a 2-quart pot or Dutch oven, making sure there is about 2 inches of oil. Using a cooking thermometer, bring the oil to 355°F. If you don't have a thermometer, heat the oil for about 15 minutes. It's ready when the oil bubbles vigorously.

6. Carefully place 1 donut or 3 donut holes in the oil and cook until browned, anywhere from 30 seconds to 1 minute 30 seconds, depending on the heat of the oil. Using a slotted spoon, gently turn each donut over and cook the other side until browned, 30 seconds to 1 minute.

7. Using the slotted spoon, remove the cooked donuts and donut holes from the oil and place them on the paper towel–lined baking sheet. Repeat with the rest of the dough quickly to prevent the oil from heating up too much between batches.

TO MAKE THE GLAZE

8. In a medium bowl, sift the confectioners' sugar. Add the milk and vanilla, and whisk until smooth.

9. Dip the donuts and donut holes into the glaze and place them onto the parchment paper–lined baking sheet. Let cool before enjoying.

This easy recipe uses baking powder to make them light and airy.

For the donuts

¼ cup canola or vegetable oil

¾ cup granulated sugar

1 cup whole milk

1 egg

¾ teaspoon vanilla

2 cups flour

1½ teaspoons baking powder

½ teaspoon baking soda

¼ teaspoon salt

½ teaspoon ground cinnamon

¼ teaspoon ground nutmeg

For the glaze

¾ cup powdered sugar

1 to 2 tablespoons milk

¼ teaspoon vanilla

For the cinnamon sugar coating

1/3 cup granulated sugar

1 teaspoon ground cinnamon

½ cup unsalted butter

TO MAKE THE DONUTS

1 Preheat the oven to 350°F. Grease a donut pan with butter and dust with flour.

2 In a small bowl, whisk together the oil, sugar, milk, egg, and vanilla. In a large bowl, mix together the flour, baking powder, baking soda, salt, cinnamon, and nutmeg.

3 Form a small well in the dry ingredients and pour in the wet ingredients, making sure to scrape down the sides to get all of the sugar. Combine with a whisk.

4 Carefully spoon about 3 tablespoons of batter into each donut cup, making sure not to fill them more than ¾ full. Bake for 10 to 15 minutes, or until a toothpick inserted into a donut comes out clean. Transfer the donuts to a wire rack to cool. Repeat using the rest of the batter.

TO MAKE THE GLAZE AND COATING

5 To make the glaze, sift the powdered sugar and mix together with 1 tablespoon of milk and the vanilla in a medium bowl, and whisk until smooth. If the mixture seems too thick, add more milk, 1 teaspoon at a time, until you get the consistency you want. Set aside.

6 To make the cinnamon sugar coating, combine the sugar and cinnamon in a medium bowl. Set aside. In a medium microwave-safe bowl, completely melt the butter in the microwave in 10 second bursts.

7 To make glazed donuts, dip each cooled donut into the glaze to cover one side. Let sit for a few minutes until set.

8 If you prefer cinnamon sugar donuts, brush one side of the donut with melted butter and then dip it into the cinnamon sugar mixture.

About the Author

Rachel Teichman is a freelance writer who loves to share cooking and crafting ideas with families. She created Crafts and Crumbs (@craftsandcrumbs) to post her favorites on social media. Rachel's debut book is *B is for Bagel*, and her work has been featured in *The Buzz Magazines*, *Kveller*, and *Red Tricycle*. She lives in Houston, Texas, with her husband and three children, and loves all of the local donut options. Her favorite donut is a glazed old-fashioned.

Acknowledgments

Rebecca Wright, for showcasing all of the sprinkles, sugar, and jelly that donuts have to offer.

The Collective Book Studio and Book Buddy teams, for making this book the best version of itself.

Like Minds Talk, for always having great ideas.

The Sunny La La for the cool merch and more.

Emily, for grocery store donut outings.

My friends and family, for your sweet support of my round food obsession.

Nina, for all of our brunches, my IG logos, and your The Fakery Co. inspiration.

Eli, for gathering all of the donuts with me, and making the Key Lime one happen.

Ezra, for all of our morning donut runs.

Jesse—a chocolate cake donut, right?

For more D is for Donut content visit www.craftsncrumbs.com

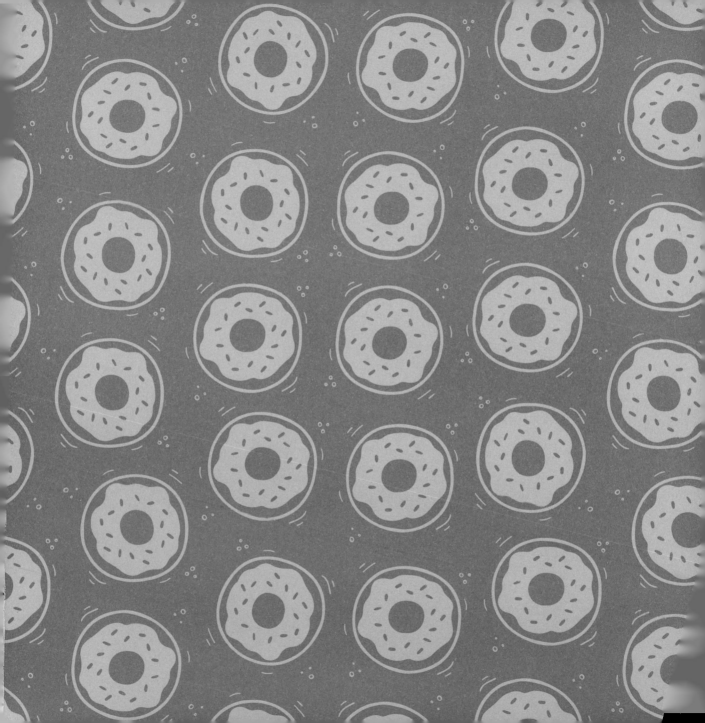

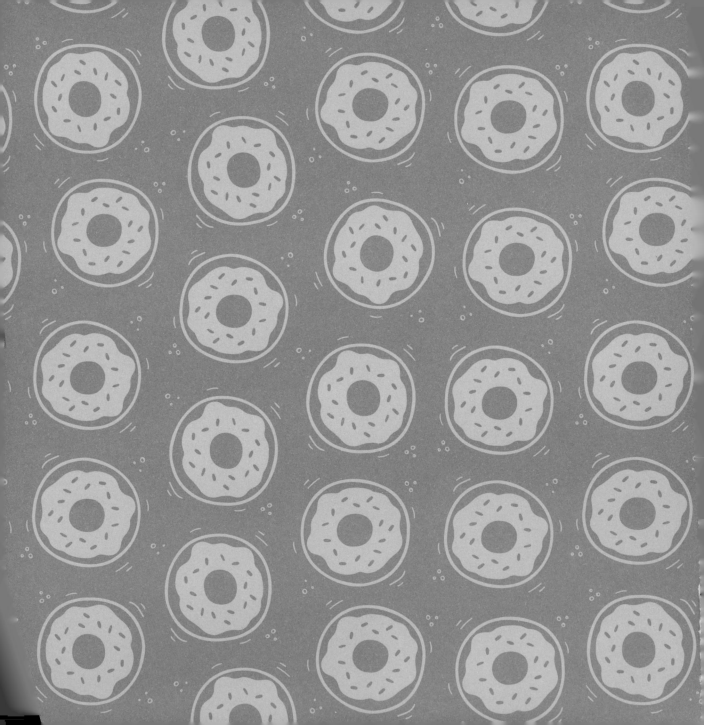